Space for God

LEADER'S GUIDE

by Don Postema

CRC Publications
Grand Rapids, Michigan

Space for God: Study and Practice of Spirituality and Prayer, Leader's Guide, © 1983, 1997, CRC Publications, 2850 Kalamazoo Ave. SE, Grand Rapids, MI 49560. All rights reserved. With the exception of brief excerpts for review purposes, no part of this book may be reproduced in any manner whatsoever without written permission from the publisher. Printed in the United States of America on recycled paper. ⊕ 1-800-333-8300

ISBN 0-933140-47-9

9 8 7 6 5 4 3 2

CONTENTS

  *Note: Textbook is handed out during the introductory session and chapter 1 of text assigned as home reading.
 **Note: There is no corresponding textbook chapter for session 10.

INTRODUCTION

To the Leader:

I would like to sit down with you in a quiet place and talk about leading this course. Better yet, I'd like to take a walk with you in a woods, stop by a stream, and be aware of God's presence as we converse about the spiritual life, prayer, and how it all fits into our overcrowded lives. Since I can't do that personally, I'm using this small leader's guide as a way to talk with you about leading the course.

When I was first asked to lead a retreat on prayer, I was a bit intimidated. The retreat was for a group of pastors and their spouses, and I was sure they knew more about the spiritual life and prayer than I did! Since I felt I couldn't go to the retreat as a "leader," much less as an "expert," I went as a fellow-learner. I think that if you approach "leading" this course as a learner, along with other learners, you'll have a much easier time of it.

The suggestions I offer for each session come from my experience of teaching this material over many years. I am sure there are other ways to use this material, and I would be happy to have you try your ideas as well as mine. Please regard what I say as more of a guide than a prescription. As you become more familiar with the people in the group and with the course, you'll know what needs to be emphasized and what needs to be changed.

I suggest you become familiar with the whole course before attempting to lead others through it. Reading through the textbook and leader's guide will give you a sense of where the course is heading. The major goal of the course is to help each person write—and faithfully carry out—a personal prayer discipline (see session 6). The course is also intended to give participants some theological basis, some personal exercises, some readings and art, some understanding and experience of spirituality and prayer that can lead to that personal practice of prayer.

Underlying this approach is the belief that we can learn *about* prayer (from a wide variety of religious traditions) and that we also can learn *how* to pray. I used to think that we learned how to pray by osmosis—from the way our parents, our pastors, our teachers, or our relatives prayed. And if we weren't very good at it—well, there just wasn't much we could do about it. I no longer believe that. When people say, "Teach us to pray," I believe we can show them how. This course attempts to teach a few ways of praying. There are, of course, many other ways that are not included—ways and traditions that you may want to explore on your own. In the end no method guarantees leading us into the perfect way to pray, no method removes all difficulties and obstacles. Thomas Merton, in *Contemplative Prayer,* suggests that we not look for a method or system of prayer, but cultivate an attitude—an outlook of faith, openness, attention, reverence, expectation, supplication, trust, joy.

This course offers some humble suggestions to help you lead others to their own personal way of being aware of God, of speaking with God, of living their lives of love and justice in the presence of divine majesty, mystery, and mercy. Perhaps all we can do is remove some barriers so God can come to us.

To help you lead your group, I've included some reactions and questions from groups I've led. These reactions generally show the need to deal sensitively and gently with a wide range of responses. Because the material encourages a very personal exploration of our relationship to God, you can expect very diverse and even contradictory responses. Our prayer lives should be as personal as our toothbrushes. And since there is no one "right way" to experience God, to interact with God's holy Presence, we can be enriched and stretched by each person's experiences and understanding. The best part about being the leader is the opportunity it will give you to learn from the people in your group. You'll probably find yourself saying, more than once or twice, "I never thought of that before!" Stay with these ideas a while longer, be challenged by them, perhaps make them your own. Each time I teach this course, I learn something new from people. And they learn a great deal from each other too. I hope this will be your experience over the next few weeks.

I think doing the exercises a week before the group does them will help you understand people's responses. It will also allow you to speak from some, if limited, experience. When someone says, "I don't think I can do that exercise," or "What's the point of trying that?" you'll be able to offer some specific encouragement, based on your own experience. So try to stay at least a week ahead of the group.

I learned quickly that I couldn't lead by myself. As I led others, I found myself praying more intensely, "Lord, teach *me* to pray!" You, too, will need to be in touch with God, into whose Presence you are leading others. I hope your thoughts will be focused more on prayer during these weeks, and that you will be praying more. As you and your group ask the Lord to teach you to pray, may the Spirit give you insight and sensitivity and courage. May you become more deeply aware of the wonder of God's gracious Presence and grasp the depth of life the resurrected Christ has opened for you.

Don Postema
Easter, 1983

SECOND EDITION NOTES

This second edition of the *Space for God* leader's guide incorporates references to whatever is new in the second edition of the *Space for God* textbook, especially expanded or additional prayer exercises.

During the fourteen years since *Space for God* was first published, many people have spoken to me about their experiences in leading this course. I'm thankful that many leaders have said this guide is helpful.

I must say that I never envisioned this course being taught in so many different situations. One person uses it with cancer patients, another in a summer program with teens, another with prison inmates, another in an inner-city church in Chicago. It has been used in seminaries and in the United States armed forces. A woman in Michigan has taught it so many times that it has become her avocation. Another woman told me she has worn out three books teaching it. How gratifying to see how a book can find its way into the lives of so many different kinds of people!

This course and its teaching approach was an experiment in 1983. Introducing a topic at one session, reading about it during the week, reviewing it at the next session, doing prayer exercises and discussing them . . . all these things give people a continuous experience throughout the week and throughout the course. Participants are urged not only to read about the spiritual life but to develop their own spirituality, not only to talk about prayer but to pray, not only to think about God but to experience God.

In *Reformed Spirituality*, Howard Rice indicates that people in the Reformed tradition have often been ambivalent about the role of experience in the Christian life. Even though our spiritual ancestor, John Calvin, insisted that the Christian life consisted of *experience* of God as well as *knowledge* of God and *service* to God, we tend to choose knowledge as the way to relate to God. Rather than trust our religious feelings as a way to "truth" about God, we tend to trust our minds much more.

But—as my learned friend Lewis Smedes taught me—"when it comes to God, our minds are as tricky as our feelings. I know that my brains have often made a fool out of me with God. Early on, I conned myself into supposing that if I had a clear head focused on a clear doctrine of divine grace, I would actually be experiencing grace" (*How Can It Be All Right When Everything Is All Wrong?*). We often act as though theology is a workable substitute for experience. Yet we need both! According to John Calvin, we have knowledge of God when we know facts about God *and* have an actual acquaintance with God.

Space for God tries to bring together both aspects of the Reformed tradition: theology and piety, knowledge and experience. It is meant to foster what I call *experiential knowledge,* which encourages people to love God with their whole heart as well as with their whole mind, with their ideas as well as with their feelings. Chapter 5 explores this spirituality of mind and heart in detail, but it is really the presupposition of the entire book and course. I have become more convinced of it as I continue to study, teach, and pray. Many people tell me they have been blessed and inspired by this approach.

So I encourage you as leader to help your group members stay with their experiences as they read, discuss, and pray their way through this course. Even their experience of ideas! It's very easy to drift into a discussion of our ideas and forget about our experiences. You as leader can help people learn with and from both mind and heart. As you keep that focus during each session, I pray that you will have a rich experience of God with your group.

—Don Postema
Epiphany, 1997

P.S. Since the first edition of *Space for God* was published, more books have appeared on the subject of spirituality and spiritual practice from a Reformed perspective—the main tradition that informs this course. Let me mention several books you might use for reference, for additional insight as you teach, and for future study by your group:

Reformed Spirituality: An Introduction for Believers by
   Howard L. Rice, Westminster/John Knox Press,
   Louisville, Kentucky, 1991.
Soul Feast: An Invitation to the Christian Spiritual Life
   by Marjorie J. Thompson, Westminster/John Knox
   Press, Louisville, Kentucky, 1995.

In addition, CRC Publications has a number of
books in a new series on spiritual growth. These
resources are for small groups or individual study.
They include:

Catch Your Breath: God's Invitation to Sabbath Rest by
   Don Postema
*Celebrating God's Presence: The Transforming Power of
   Public Worship* by Tom Schwanda
Finding Our Way to God: A Pilgrimage with the Psalms
   by Harvey Stob
Guiding the Faith Journey: A Map for Spiritual Leaders
   by Neil deKoning
More Than Words: Prayer as a Way of Life by Leonard J.
   Vander Zee
Patterns for Prayer: 52 Weeks of Prayer Ideas

Please contact CRC Publications for additional
titles.

ADDITIONAL INFORMATION FOR LEADERS

Organization of the Course

The first four sessions focus on spirituality and the basis for prayer. What biblical and theological concepts, what personal attitudes and feelings should we cultivate as we come to God in prayer? Attitudes of leisure, of belonging to God, of gratitude, and of awareness are examined. Session and home exercises help participants explore these concepts, develop these attitudes, and begin to practice regular prayer at home.

The fifth session moves from the general area of spirituality to the more specific area of prayer, looking at prayer as an attitude of a receptive heart. The remaining five sessions focus on prayer as an act: How do we go about praying? When and where can we pray? What can we include in our prayers? What is the goal of our prayers? The exercises turn specifically toward the development and practice of a personal prayer discipline.

Organization of Each Session

Session 1 is something of an introduction to the course. It will give you the opportunity to explain what the course is about, to hand out the textbook, to assign the reading of chapter 1 and a beginning At Home exercise.

The next meeting, session 2, takes a "look back" at group members' reactions to chapter 1 and the At Home exercises assigned during the previous session. Session 2 also "looks ahead" to chapter 2. An In Session exercise is completed and an At Home exercise, including the reading of chapter 2, is assigned. That's the basic pattern of all the sessions in this course: a look back to the previous chapter and its At Home exercise; a look ahead to the next chapter and assignment of its At Home exercise. As the weeks go by, the content of the At Home exercises increases until group members finally write and practice their own prayer disciplines.

Each session also includes opening prayers (both silent and spoken) as well as closing prayers.

Time

Most of the sessions outlined in this guide are planned to take about an hour each; in fact, you'll be most comfortable with about an hour and a half for each session. Holding your meetings on a weekday or evening, rather than on Sunday after or before church, will give you more flexibility on the length of the sessions.

The ten-session format is certainly flexible; for example, I've done the course in six longer, two-hour sessions, as follows:

Session 1—Chapters 1 and 2
Session 2—Chapters 3 and 5
Session 3—Chapters 4 and 6
Session 4—Chapter 7
Session 5—Chapter 8
Session 6—Chapter 9

Sometimes I'm asked to give a single presentation of an hour and a half or so. To do that, I combine chapters 1 and 2, using just enough from chapter 1 to show the difficulty but necessity of taking time for prayer. Then I talk briefly about belonging and have the group do the In Session exercise from chapter 2 (contemplating the Prodigal Son). I introduce gratitude as a response to belonging to God, using the exercise "I am thankful for . . . " (the In Session exercise of chapter 3). That gives people a five-minute prayer for morning and evening (see At Home exercise for chapter 3). If you're a pastor, you could even boil this down to sermon length, ending your sermon by having people spend some time in silence saying, "I belong to God." The next sermon (perhaps on Thanksgiving Day) can use the "I am thankful for . . . " exercise.

I hope you can see from the above that, while the course is designed for ten 60-90 minute sessions, it can be used in many other ways as well.

Group Size and Meeting Place

I think you'll get the best results if you limit the group size to around twelve. I'm talking now about regular sessions, not a short presentation (such as described above) or a retreat. A dozen, give or take a few, will give you good discussion and interaction; it will allow you to meet in a normal-sized room at church or in homes.

It really doesn't matter if you meet at church or at home. What matters is providing a place where people can be reasonably comfortable and where a certain amount of quietness can be assured so times of silence won't be interrupted. It's helpful if the room has movable chairs and is spacious enough to allow for some small group work and at least a measure of individual privacy for meditating, writing in journals, and so on. Avoid the formal classroom setup, with people sitting in rows and you at the front; instead, arrange the chairs in a circle or semicircle and sit with the group.

A chalkboard or large pad of newsprint and markers are necessary for several of the sessions. Also, a cassette player for music and/or a small bell are effective for beginning and ending times of silence. It's a good idea to keep a supply of writing paper in the room for those who forget their journals. Extra pens and pencils come in handy as well.

Most of the Scripture selections and hymns used in the sessions can be found in Windows to Insight in the textbook.

Journals

Each participant (including you as leader) should keep a journal for writing out the exercises, for writing prayers, for jotting down questions and reactions to the chapters, and for keeping an account of his or her experiences. Encourage everybody to bring in the journals (and textbooks) to each meeting.

It will help if you bring notebooks to the first session meeting and sell them to group members. That way, no one will lag behind in purchasing and using a journal.

Music

I've found that the use of a good cassette player and appropriate music adds a certain dignity and reverence to the sessions. Playing soft music is a gentle way to begin and end the many times of silence that this course suggests. No doubt you have your own ideas about what kind of music to use. I personally have made use of a mix of classical, light classical, and folk. In the Windows to Insight for each chapter you'll find a number of hymns and psalms.

Don't think that you have to have an elaborate array of recorded music to make this course successful. You can just as well ask your group to sing; in fact, you could pick one hymn to begin your times of meditation and another hymn to end them. Sing a few bars and ask the group to join you. In no time at all, you'll have a very lovely and effective way of beginning and ending your times of silence.

With this updated edition of *Space for God*, CRC Publications has released a new recording: *Space for God in Words and Music.* For you and the members of your group, the recording can serve as a reminder of what you've learned and an incentive for continuing the individual prayer disciplines you've begun.

Reminders

As I prepare for each session, I remind myself of a few things. Maybe my list will be helpful to you. First, I remember that each person in the group is a gift to me, to other participants, and to himself or herself; therefore each person's comments, responses, and questions are a gift, and I need to encourage myself and each group member to listen to others and to themselves.

I remind myself that I need to keep from defensiveness and arguing and that I need to learn to listen for understanding. I need to affirm people in what they are trying to express, to assure them it's OK to have a different point of view than the textbook or others in the group. I need to learn about prayer from others in the group.

I remind myself to refrain from commenting on everything that people say. I should allow statements to stand without comment, so that others can respond to them. And I must give people a chance to be wordless, quiet.

God helping me, I should act out what I teach, so that people experience belonging and acceptance, compassion and joy and thankfulness. I pray that God will help me show others what it means to be in God's presence, if only for a few minutes. I don't want to send people home more hassled and competitive than when they came.

These are the attitudes I try to have as I lead. They have helped me keep a perspective on what's happening. You may find it helpful to write down some attitudes you want to have when you lead. Then review your list just before class time.

Retreats

A retreat can be a relaxing setting for learning about spirituality and prayer. It's often easier to meditate away from the busyness of the daily routine. On the other hand, participants will not have the time to practice the exercises at home, as they would during the regular ten-week course. And you'll have to be very familiar with the material if you hope to fit it all into a compact plan for a retreat.

I often hold retreats in the middle of a course or at its end. For example, the group will have regular meetings for sessions 1-4; then we'll do sessions 5-7 on a Saturday morning and afternoon retreat (or Sunday afternoon and evening). Then we'll continue with sessions 8-10 in regular meetings. A variation of this is to hold regular meetings for sessions 1-6, then finish sessions 7-10 on retreat.

Following is a plan for a Friday night/Saturday retreat that enables groups to experience much of the regular *Space for God* course. Of course, this is only one way to do it. You will want to modify my plan to suit your own situation.

Note: All chapter references refer to chapters in the *Space for God* textbook.

FRIDAY NIGHT

7:00 Presentation on the difficulty/necessity of making space for God (chapter 1). Also a chance to be quiet, with some music and Scripture readings. Brief silence, ending with Thomas Merton prayer.

7:30 Discussion of the above.

7:50 Presentation of belonging to God as the basis for spirituality and prayer (chapter 2).

8:15 Exercise from chapter 2: Contemplation of the parable of the prodigal son.

8:30 Discussion of the above exercise.

9:00 Evening prayers.

SATURDAY

7:30 Silence. Then morning prayers as a group.

8:00 Breakfast.

9:00 Presentation of "Gratitude Takes Nothing for Granted" from chapter 3.

9:20 Exercise from chapter 3: "I am thankful for . . . "

9:30 Discussion of above exercise.

10:00 Break.

10:20 Presentation of "Gestures of Gratitude" (chapter 4).

10:40 Chapter 4 exercise: Contemplation of the story of the ten lepers.

11:00 Discussion of above exercise. Why did you return? Why didn't you return? Listing of personal gestures of gratitude.

11:45 Lunch.

1:00 Presentation of "Prayer as Attitude: The Grateful Heart" (chapter 5).

1:20 Chapter 5 exercise: What is prayer to me?

1:30 Discussion of above exercise.

2:00 Presentation of "Prayer as Act" (chapter 6).

2:30 Chapter 6 exercise: Writing a personal prayer discipline. Important for all to do.

3:00 Break.

3:20 Presentation of "The Goal Is Glory" (chapter 9).

3:40 Chapter 9 exercise: Contemplate the account of the transfiguration of Christ.

4:00 Discussion of above exercise.

4:30 Closing prayer and worship.

5:00 Leave for home.

If your retreat runs through Saturday evening, modify the Saturday schedule as follows:

SATURDAY

1:00 Presentation of "Prayer as Attitude: The Grateful Heart" (chapter 5).

1:20 Chapter 5 exercise: What is prayer to me?
1:30 Discussion of above exercise.
2:00 Chapter 5 exercise: To whom do you pray?
2:10 Discussion of above exercise.
2:45 Break.
3:00 Presentation of "Prayer as Act" (chapter 6).
3:30 Chapter 6 exercise: Writing a personal prayer discipline.
4:00 Discussion of above exercise.
4:30 Break.
5:30 Dinner.
6:30 Presentation of "Wrestling with God" (chapter 7) or "Prayer and Justice/ Compassion" (chapter 8).
7:00 Chapter 7 exercise: Writing a psalm of complaint. Or chapter 8 exercise: Praying prayers of justice and compassion.
7:15 Discussion of above exercise.
8:00 Break.
8:15 Presentation of "The Goal Is Glory" (chapter 9).
9:00 Closing worship.

If your retreat continues through Sunday noon, you will be able to include all the chapters, as follows:

SATURDAY NIGHT

6:30 Presentation of chapter 7.
7:00 Chapter 7 exercise: Writing a psalm of complaint.
7:20 Discussion of above exercise.
8:15 Evening prayers.
8:35 Break for rest of evening.

SUNDAY MORNING

7:30 Morning prayers.
8:00 Breakfast.
8:45 Presentation of "Prayer and Justice/Compassion" (chapter 8).
9:15 Chapter 8 exercise: Praying prayers of justice and compassion.
9:30 Discussion.
10:00 Break.
10:30 Closing worship, including chapter 9.
11:45 Lunch, and leave for home.

Note: I've allowed a fair amount of time in these schedules for discussion, interaction, and breaks. You don't want people to feel hassled during a retreat! So be flexible. If your group gets into any extended discussions or if they're showing signs of weariness, cut back on one or more of the scheduled events.

SESSION 1
(INTRODUCTORY SESSION)

MAKING SPACE

PURPOSE

This first session introduces us to the textbook and the course, to the concept of spirituality, to the discipline of prayer, and to the theme of chapter 1— our need to make space for God in our lives.

Note: Hand out the textbook at this first session. Group members will be asked to read chapter 1 at home after this introductory session.

PRAYER   *(2-4 minutes)*

As you would expect in a course about prayer and spirituality, each session is conducted in the context of prayer, beginning and ending with prayers. These opening prayers should consist of a time of silence followed by a spoken prayer (by you or a group member). It's important that all group members be present for the opening prayer for all sessions.

Don't wait until later in the course to begin praying—start today's session with prayer. That way you'll be establishing an opening procedure and beginning a "discipline" of prayer. How you begin this session sets the tone for the session and perhaps for the entire course.

Silence   *(1-2 minutes)*

Simply ask everyone to be silent for one minute— to focus on being present before God in this group. Tell them how long the prayer will be so they won't wonder when it will end. Conclude the time of silence by going directly into the spoken prayer.

It's a good idea to ask participants to arrive five minutes early from now on. They should sit in silence until the session begins. I do this with my groups, and it helps people to "center" or "focus" themselves. It gives them a chance to put their busyness behind

them and to be sensitive to the people in the group, to the subject at hand, to themselves, and to God. Of course, this takes longer than one minute. But at first one minute will seem like a long time to people who aren't used to silence. You will be increasing the time for silence each week so group members will gradually grow accustomed to it.

Now you can see why it's important that people arrive on time or even a little early—so they can participate in the silence and so they will not disturb the silence of others by walking in late. Sometimes the group discusses later what happened during the silence; coming late could mean missing an important part of such discussion.

For the first session or two, you may want to put a sign on the door or quietly remind people to please enter in silence. Otherwise interruptions will ruin the time of silence. By the way, the room where you meet should be somewhat secluded and sheltered from adjoining noise.

Spoken Prayer   *(1-2 minutes)*

This prayer should lead people into the presence of God and into an awareness of the topic of the day. You can use your own words or those of Psalm 42 (see Windows, chapter 1). Another possibility is the following prayer from Thomas Merton:

My Lord God,
I have no idea where I am going.
I do not see the road ahead of me.
I cannot know for certain where it will end.
Nor do I really know myself,
And the fact that I think I am following your will does not mean that I am actually doing so.
But I believe that the desire to please you does in fact please you.

And I hope I have that desire in all that I am doing.
I hope that I will never do anything apart from that
desire.
And I know that if I do this, you will lead me by the
right road though I may know nothing about it.
Therefore I will trust you always though I may seem to
be lost and in the shadow of death.
I will not fear, for you are ever with me,
And you will never leave me to face my perils alone.
— Thomas Merton, *Thoughts in Solitude*, p. 83

INTRODUCING
THE COURSE   *(15-20 minutes)*

Hand out nametags, but consider dispensing with the usual introductory speeches. I like to have people think of each other first of all as people interested in prayer and spirituality, not as people who come from certain backgrounds, work at certain jobs or professions, and so on. Group members can learn these facts later as they gradually come to know each other. I find that even if people are well acquainted at the beginning of the course, they come to see one another in a new light.

It does help to have people say their name whenever they speak, at least for the first few sessions. By listening carefully to names and comments, group members will come to know each other as time goes by.

To get things started, you might want to say something along these lines (but please use your own words, not mine!):

I commend you for being here, for wanting to deepen your spiritual life and enrich your praying. I believe that taking this kind of time is not a luxury but a necessity if we are going to live our lives in depth and grow spiritually. I know I need that. Perhaps you do too.

In this course we'll be reading, thinking, and talking about prayer, but we'll also be praying.

Some of you may already have a prayer-full life but may want to enrich it; others may feel inadequate as pray-ers. All of us are here as learners together. (You can pause here and ask people to explain why they are taking the course.)

I hope we're not in competition here, trying to see who can be the best pray-er. I hope we won't be intimidated by anyone who is in a different place than we are. As Thomas Merton writes, "We will never be anything else but beginners."

So let's begin . . .

Distribute the textbooks and page through chapter 1 with the class, pointing out the structure of the book. A handy guide to each chapter's structure is found after the first Reflection. Be careful not to consume too much time going through this introduction to the book; it's really important that you get to the next section of this lesson, Looking Ahead.

As you page through the Reflection with the class, you might call attention to some of the goal statements found there:

— to deepen your life and your prayers
— to learn some ways to pray
— to develop a discipline of prayer

Be sure students understand they're to read the Reflection section of chapter 1 for next time.

Briefly explain the function of Windows to Insight, perhaps using the comments printed after the Reflection. Note that part of the work at home this week is to reflect on these Windows for ten minutes a day.

When you look at the exercise section, stress the importance of doing the exercises faithfully. Explain also that students should keep a journal. (If possible, bring a supply of ordinary notebooks to this first session. If participants can purchase their "journals" from you, they will be able to begin immediately.) Keeping a journal provides an invaluable incentive and resource for group discussion and eliminates writing in the textbook. Encourage group members to bring their journals to class each week and use them for reference. Since very shy people can read something they wrote, the journals should improve discussion. (Naturally some journal entries are private and should be kept that way.) Explain that people can use journals for answers to exercises, reactions to materials, personal prayers, and personal notes.

Conclude by briefly explaining the structure of the sessions. Note that the sessions center on the exercises. Each session looks back on what was done at home during the week and forward to the next chapter and the next set of exercises. Tell the group that reading the chapters and doing the exercises is basic to the success of the course.

Take a moment to comment on expectations for group discussion. You may want to say something like this:

During our discussions I encourage you to listen to each other—not first of all to agree or disagree, but to understand each other. Let another person's thought or experience into your imagination for a while. Try to enter into her experience. Above all, listen *rather than think about you are going to say next. That may mean silences between the times we speak. That's OK. I will try to respect those silences. I hope you will too. Not everyone needs to speak, but I will try to give everyone the opportunity to do so.*

LOOKING AHEAD   (10 minutes)

Spend the remainder of class time giving everyone a little taste of what's ahead in chapter 1. Have the class turn to the last paragraph on page 16: "To live so deeply is a special challenge, for it is so easy to be superficial." After reading that paragraph, read a few biblical texts aloud, so that everyone will be thinking about the same Scripture. Suggestions:

—Psalm 42:1-2 (see Windows)
—Mark 1:35; 6:31; 3:20-21 (these passages tell of Jesus finding time for solitude and prayer, despite his frantic pace)

Comment that if Jesus needed to take time to be alone with God, we certainly do too! You might use this remark from Luther: "I have so much business I cannot get on without spending three hours daily in prayer." If you wish, talk with the group about your own need for solitude and prayer.

EXERCISES   (15-20 minutes)

In Session

Read the In Session exercise on page 32 of the text, then invite group members to reflect on their experiences. How busy are they? Is it easy or hard for them to find time to pray?

Ask group members to write down some hindrances to prayer or the spiritual life that they have experienced: activities, thoughts, ideas, attitudes, and feelings that keep them from spending time with God. Many of the things they write will probably not be "bad" things, just things that take priority in their day.

After a few minutes of writing, ask for volunteers to share their thoughts. Talk about the kind of things we may need to reexamine so that we can make more time and space for God in our lives.

This discussion leads into the At Home exercise.

At Home

Even though you've already looked at the At Home exercise for chapter 1, take a minute now to make sure everyone understands that the exercise is their assignment for next time. The exercise calls for reading and reflecting on chapter 1 for ten to fifteen minutes a day, as well as deciding on a time and place for such reflection and for morning prayer.

If you purchased notebooks (journals) for group members, hand them out now; if not, encourage everyone to go out and buy a journal soon! Remind your group to bring their textbooks and their journals to the next session—and to come a little early.

PRAYER   (5 minutes)

Conclude the session by reading the poem "Covenant" to the group (see p. 27 of text).

Close with prayer, asking for the courage to answer God's invitation to make space in your lives for the divine Presence. Ask for the guidance of the Spirit as you begin this course.

If time permits, sing "Take Time to Be Holy" from page 28 of the textbook.

SESSION 2

I BELONG

PURPOSE

This second session begins with a look back, asking us to comment on our experiences with chapter 1 and its exercise. The remainder of the session looks ahead to chapter 2, helping us realize that the basis for the Christian life—and thus of spirituality, piety, and prayer—is the belief in and experience of belonging to God.

PRAYER   (4-5 minutes)

Silence   (3 minutes)

Ring a soft bell to let people know when the silence begins. Move directly from the silence into the spoken prayer.

Spoken Prayer   (1-2 minutes)

Use this prayer or one of your own:

O silent God,
we receive these few minutes of quiet
as a gift from you in our noisy day.
Thank you.

And because time is so precious to us,
we offer these few moments of solitude
as a total gift of ourselves to you.

O listening God,
hear our prayers,
hear our unspoken needs,
hear our discussion.

O speaking God,
may your Word come to us
through our words together.
                              Amen.

LOOKING BACK   (10-15 minutes)

The purpose of this section—which will appear in every session—is to solicit reactions to what class members read, thought, and did (related to the exercises and to prayer) during the past week. To get things started today you could say something like this (using your own words, of course):

You have been reading and reflecting this past week. What were your thoughts and experiences? I'm not asking right now what your questions are, but rather what your personal reactions were to chapter 1 and the exercises. Did you, for example, set aside a time and place for prayer?

There's no right or wrong way to respond; each person will probably have different reactions. Use whatever you have written in your journals as a reminder of your experiences.

Remember, we are all beginners, all learners. We need time to learn to listen to each other. It's OK if your point of view differs from the textbook and from others in the group. Let's try to think of each comment as a gift. When people speak, try to listen in order to understand. Don't think of whether you agree or disagree, and don't try to think of answers to their remarks. Most of all, try not to be formulating your own speech. Simply listen and respond to what the person says with a comment, a question, or an experience of your own that may be similar or different.

Let's hear what you have to say . . .

As leader, set the tone by being calm and easy with silences. If no one says anything for half a minute, be patient. It takes time to learn not to be anxious about silence. If some individuals are especially shy and withdrawn, you may want to encourage them by gently inviting their comments. But don't force participation. Remember, too, that it's best to avoid arguments and defensiveness as you explore such a personal and delicate area as one's prayer life. How you listen and respond to each person is important in creating an atmosphere and attitude of acceptance.

Sometimes people will respond in purely impersonal, intellectual ways. When that happens, I often say something like this: "That's an interesting comment; can you explain what it means to you personally?" If you don't understand the comment, you may want to help the person clarify what was said.

The session will soon turn to the idea of belonging (chapter 2). You can help people feel a real sense of belonging by cultivating the gift of listening and by encouraging them to participate. Saying "thank you" after each comment is also encouraging.

LOOKING AHEAD (10-15 minutes)

The purpose of this section—which will appear in each session—is to help the group move into the next chapter (chapter 2) and its topic. As leader, you'll probably be doing most of the talking, though if you have time, be sure to encourage some group discussion.

Begin by explaining that it's time to move on to chapter 2, a chapter that gives the basis for the Christian life, for spirituality, for prayer. Have the group turn to the opening paragraphs of chapter 2 and read them aloud, just to get into the idea of belonging.

You could call attention to the places (mentioned in chapter 2) where we feel we belong: home, family, school, church, and so on. Add a personal example, if you wish. If time permits, ask each person to mention one place or one relationship where they personally feel they "belong."

Chapter 2 also talks about human loneliness, times when we feel alone and isolated. You can explore that together, using personal examples. Remember you are pointing people toward the question the chapter raises: "To whom do I belong?"

Read some references from chapter 2 that discuss ways we seek to escape our loneliness. Point out that we need to "stay with" our loneliness, not run from it, in order to find out that we belong to God.

Conclude your presentation with a reading of Scripture passages that speak about belonging to God (examples: Psalm 100; Romans 14:7-8; 1 Corinthians 3:23—see Windows to Insight). You might also want to use examples from chapter 2 or Q&A 1 of the Heidelberg Catechism.

EXERCISES (25-35 minutes)

In Session

Ask the class to turn to the In Session exercise at the end of chapter 2. Read through the exercise with the group and tell them how you intend to signal the end of each section. I think it's best not to say something to end the meditation, since that tends to break the flow of thought; playing soft music or ringing a quiet bell has worked better in my groups. Also, be sure the group understands the directions for the meditation—that it's an experiential, not an exegetical, exercise. This is also a time for your group members to give themselves the gift of silence during the fifteen minutes of meditation. Getting a cup of coffee, paging through the text, and making other noise can be distracting to the whole group. It's helpful to remind the group that they are giving each other the gift of silence.

Begin with a careful and expressive reading of the parable of the prodigal. Either read the selection yourself or have a group member prepared to do the reading. The parable should be read slowly, so the class can savor the good news it brings.

During the time of meditation, allow people to find a small space where they can have a measure of privacy. Some like to sit on the floor; others turn their chairs to the wall or retreat to the corners of the room (it helps to have a large room and a group of not more than twelve to fifteen people).

Encourage group members to write their prayers in their journals, but have a supply of paper and pencils available, just in case.

Finally, discuss the exercise, asking people to tell how they felt as the prodigal. Encourage personal reflections, not theoretical observations. You want participants to say, "I felt . . .," not "I think Jesus was teaching that. . . ." Give as much time to the discussion as possible. Even though we'll be picking this topic up again in next week's session, it's important to have some immediate reaction to this exercise.

At Home

Review the At Home exercise for this week (see end of chapter 2). Note the procedure we're following in this course: we read a chapter at home; the following session first looks back at that chapter and its At Home exercise, then ahead at the next chapter and its exercises.

PRAYER *(5 minutes)*

To close today's session, you could ask volunteers to read the prayer they wrote for today's In Session exercise. Or you could read "A Parable of Prayer" from page 49 of the textbook. Another possibility is to sing "Nearer, Still Nearer" (see p. 41). Be sure to leave enough time for closing with a prayer or hymn. It's important that people do not simply rush out.

SESSION 3

GRATITUDE TAKES NOTHING FOR GRANTED

PURPOSE

The first part of the session focuses on our reflections on belonging to God, giving special attention to the exercise of beginning each day by saying, "I belong to God."

The second part of the session points us toward gratitude as a response to belonging and as the heart of the Christian life. God makes space for us in the covenant family. We make space for God by responding in thankfulness. We stand ready to receive from God.

PRAYER   (6-7 minutes)

Silence   (5 minutes)

By now people should be arriving on time and in silence. Ring a bell to signal the beginning of class and of five minutes of silence. If you prefer, introduce this time of silence by reading Psalm 95:1-3, 6-7 (found in Windows) or another text of thanksgiving.

Spoken Prayer   (1-2 minutes)

Again, use your own prayer, the words of a psalm (see Windows), or the following prayer:

> *We give you thanks, O God,*
> *for this day.*
> *We belong to you,*
> *and that gives us comfort and confidence.*
> *You shower us with blessings,*
> *and that inspires praise and prayer.*
> *You are always present with us,*
> *and that fills us with awe and wonder.*
> *Open our eyes, our minds, our hearts,*
> *so that we may be present to you*
> *and to each other.*
> *In the name of Jesus our Savior,*
>
> > *Amen.*

LOOKING BACK   (20 minutes)

Group members have been reading, reflecting, writing, and praying at home during the past week. This is a chance to discuss what happened. I find this a very fascinating time. I hope your group members are willing to relate their experiences. That's how we learn from each other—by describing our difficulties and joys and expressing our needs for the future.

Introduce this time of sharing with words like these:

> *We began this course by talking about how busy our lives are and how each of us should try to find time for reading, reflection, and prayer. This past week we've been doing these very things.*
>
> *Let's talk about our experiences, especially about what happened during the time of silence, when we said, "I belong to God."*
>
> *Please feel free to describe what happened—whether it was positive or negative. Then we can discover what our needs are and discuss how to meet them.*

Some things people have said:

> *It felt too mechanical to repeat one phrase.*
> *I thought we had been warned against "vain repetition" by the Bible. (The emphasis, I think, is on* vain, *not on* repetition.)
> *The phrase got trite after a while. Why this phrase and not another? (Any phrase that summarizes in a few words a person's concept or experience of God could be used: "The Lord is my Shepherd," "God is Love," "God is my refuge and strength," etc.)*
> *Sounds more like a slogan than a prayer.*
> *I find it more personal to say: "I belong to you, O God."*
> *I thought it was silly just to sit and do nothing.*

*I set the clock early, sat in bed, and said it. I concen-
trated on God. It helped me establish my whole day.*

*Am I doing it right? The way the leader or the book
wants me to do it?*

*Was I supposed to say it out loud? Quietly? In my
head?*

*I found the phrase popping up at other times during the
day. (That's the ideal! It can become the background
music for our lives; a phrase that comes to mind
when we have a few moments of quiet—at a stop-
light, in line at the store, doing dishes, jogging.)*

*I imagined myself saying it in my room; then shouting it
in a football stadium full of people. I went back and
forth between my room and the stadium saying: "I
belong to God."*

*It kept getting later and later for me each day to find
time to pray.*

I couldn't find the time.

I felt relaxed.

I was moved to praise.

*I turned the phrase to "We belong to God" so I could
include more people.*

I felt like God was in charge of my day.

It gave me peace. No matter what, I was taken care of.

It took away the fear of the day.

*I resisted. It was too much like "meditation" I had done.
It was unpleasant for me.*

*It was hard to do with so many people in my house. I
was embarrassed to be saying something for five
minutes out loud.*

Hard to keep my mind from drifting.

*Nothing happened. I don't know what's supposed to
happen.*

Over the years, people have told me how they've
used the simple "I belong to God" prayer. Quite a few
people reported being comforted by the prayer as
they were going into surgery. One woman stitched "I
belong to God" on bookmarks and gave them to her
small group as a daily reminder. One high school stu-
dent who usually gets good grades was disappointed
by a C on a paper. But then she began asking herself
where she found her real comfort in life. She began
repeating "I belong to God!" It helped her rearrange
her priorities and realize that though grades were

important, they did not provide the deepest meaning
of her life.

As you listen to your group members describe
their experience with this prayer and with silence,
you may want to address some of their concerns. It's
important that group members should not feel dis-
couraged, but should realize that what happens to
them happens to most people. That's one reason why
so much has been written about silence. To guide
your discussion you could read some of the comments on silence from the Reflection and Windows of
chapter 5. These passages urge different uses of
silence: emptying the mind, filling the mind with
God's good deeds, and so on.

You might encourage people by talking about your
own experiences with silence. Remind the group that
when we are close to a friend or spouse, we don't
always have to speak. Sometimes we can be silent
together—walking, sitting in a room, driving in the
car—and the silence is not empty or awkward, but
comfortable and full of love and understanding. It
takes a long time to get to this point with a person, yet
it is worth waiting for. It also takes time to get that
close to God—so close that we can be quiet and not
feel awkward in God's Presence. The problem I have
is wanting this to happen fast! I want to learn and
experience things in a few weeks that other people
have learned over years of patient discipline.

Some in your group may have had trouble with the
phrase "I belong to God." This may not be the phrase
each person would choose as her own focusing
words. I chose it because it summarizes the content of
chapter 2, the essence of the Heidelberg Catechism
(Q&A 1), the thrust of the Bible, and a basis of the
Christian life. I suggest that people stick with these
words for a few more weeks, perhaps with a variation
such as "I belong to you, O God." Later on people
may find and use a phrase that more deeply expresses
their personal belief and experience of God. This
course is not meant to legislate what people say, but
to help them find the way of prayer that best
enhances their relationship with God. Still, I recom-
mend that group members stick to something similar
for a few weeks so that they can learn from each
other's experiences. By session 6 they will be choos-
ing a more personal style.

Others in your group may be worried about "doing it right." Accept how each person uses the phrase, and encourage him to continue. I think it's necessary to say the phrase slowly while breathing naturally. If you let the words follow your natural rhythm of breathing, you'll be reminded of them throughout the day. As you breathe, the words will form naturally with your rhythm.

Some people may also wonder about how they are supposed to "feel." I find Thomas Merton's remark helpful. "We should not judge the value of our meditation by 'how we feel.'" As I explain in chapter 5, prayer is not meant first of all to make us feel good, but to center our thoughts, hearts, and lives on God; to make us more aware that we live in God's presence; and to challenge us to live out of that awareness each day. If we feel good, so much the better.

Finally, you may want to read these helpful words about short prayers from Henri Nouwen's *The Way of the Heart*, pages 80-83:

> In the context of our verbose culture it is significant to hear the Desert Fathers discouraging us from using too many words: "Abba Macarius was asked 'How should one pray?' The old man said, 'There is no need at all to make long discourses; it is enough to stretch out one's hand and say, "Lord, as you will, and as you know, have mercy." And if the conflict grows fiercer say: "Lord, help." He knows very well what we need and he shows us his mercy.'"
>
> . . . The quiet repetition of a single word can help us to descend with the mind into the heart. This repetition has nothing to do with magic. It is not meant to throw a spell on God or to force him into hearing us. On the contrary, a word or sentence repeated frequently can help us to concentrate, to move to the center, to create an inner stillness and thus to listen to the voice of God. When we simply try to sit silently and wait for God to speak to us, we find ourselves bombarded with endless conflicting thoughts and ideas. But when we use a very simple sentence such as "O God, come to my assistance," or "Jesus, Master, have mercy on me," or a word such as "Lord" or "Jesus," it is easier to let the many distractions pass by without being misled by them. Such a simple, easily repeated prayer can slowly empty out our crowded interior life and create the quiet space where we

can dwell with God. It can be a ladder along which we can descend into the heart and ascend to God. Our choice of words depends on our needs and the circumstances of the moment, but it is best to use words from Scripture.

> This way of simple prayer, when we are faithful to it and practice it at regular times, slowly leads us to an experience of rest and opens us to God's active presence. Moreover, we can take this prayer with us into a very busy day. When, for instance, we have spent twenty minutes in the early morning sitting in the presence of God with the words "The Lord is my Shepherd," they may slowly build a little nest for themselves in our heart and stay there for the rest of our busy day. Even while we are talking, studying, gardening, or building, the prayer can continue in our heart and keep us aware of God's ever-present guidance. The discipline is not directed toward coming to a deeper insight into what it means that God is called our Shepherd, but toward coming to the inner experience of God's shepherding action in whatever we think, say or do.

Obviously you can spend a lot of time looking back on the experiences of the first two weeks. You should decide when to break off the discussion and move on to the next section. Remind people that these concerns about meditation will be discussed again as the group continues.

LOOKING AHEAD   *(10-15 minutes)*

Make the transition to the new topic of chapter 3: gratitude. Chapter 3 flows nicely from chapter 3 (belonging) because gratitude is the response of those who belong to God. Here's how I often make the transition:

> Now we'll talk about our response to belonging. We've dealt with why we make space for God (because God makes space for us). Now we'll begin asking how we make space for God. This is really the question we'll be focusing on during the rest of this course.
>
> As we move to this next section, let's have a few moments of silence. During this time I'll read some things about gratitude as our response to God.

From chapter 3's Windows, read selections from Psalm 136, Psalm 95, and 1 Thessalonians 5, as well as the last three paragraphs of the Merton piece from *Thoughts in Solitude* (page 62). Then continue along these lines:

> *How can we make space for God? By being receptive and open. Gratitude is an attitude of receptivity. What we are trying to do is cultivate an attitude, an outlook, which prepares the way for the coming of the Lord to us and makes us aware of the presence of the Lord.*
>
> *Gratitude is a way of preparing the way of the Lord, of making space for God who makes space for us. The readings and exercises for this week are about gratitude as a basic attitude of the Christian life, as a response to belonging.*

As time permits, use whatever you wish from chapter 3 to further introduce the idea of gratitude. Chapter 3 focuses on *recognizing* that a gift has been given; chapter 4 takes up gratitude as a *response* to the gift.

EXERCISES
(15 minutes)

Lead from your presentation on gratitude into the exercises at the end of chapter 3.

In Session

I ask group members to *write* what they are thankful for because it makes thanksgiving more concrete and enables people to use their list to make a prayer. Stress that people list *immediate* reasons for thanks, not events from the distant past. Explain that you'll end the ten minutes of writing with music or a bell. Then use a simple phrase such as: "Now take your list and use it as a prayer of thanksgiving to God."

Solicit reactions to the exercise. Was it helpful? Did it promote gratitude? I've found that most people like this exercise, though ten minutes isn't really enough time to write down all the things/people/events from even one day for which they are thankful.

At Home

Read through numbers 1-3 of the At Home exercise. The group will now have something with which to end the day (evening prayers) as well as begin it. The two prayers are like bookends at either end of the day—the parenthesis between which we live. The day itself belongs to God, and we give thanks to God for it. I have found that people gradually begin looking for things during the day to write down at night.

Do stress *writing* our thanks. Writing helps keep us focused and provides a permanent record. Just think, after a week we can look back on thirty-five minutes of gratitude. After a month, think of how many written reasons there can be to give thanks!

Remind everyone to reserve ten minutes for reading during the day. Since prayers of gratitude will be part of evening prayers for the next few weeks, encourage group members to expand their written prayers to include item 4, During the Week. I have found that these prayers of thanks for nature, other people, and ourselves help us pay attention during the day. They make our gratitude specific and deepen it. In fact, what we are really doing is writing psalms of thanksgiving! (See chapter 6, p. 117, for further explanation of this way of writing psalms.)

PRAYER
(5 minutes)

For the closing prayer you could ask people to offer thanks for an item or two that they've written as part of the In Session exercise. Just go around the group once or twice, each person saying "I am thankful for. . . . " This will result in a crescendo of gratitude.

If you prefer, sing a hymn (see Windows) or lead in a closing prayer of your own.

SESSION 4

GESTURES OF GRATITUDE

PURPOSE

Session 4 looks back on our experiences with morning/evening prayers, and especially with listing things for which to give thanks. The goal is to cultivate a continual attitude of thanksgiving.

The session then introduces gestures of gratitude as our response to God's love. To experience what it's like to forget expressions of thanks and to give expressions of thanks, we contemplate the story of the ten lepers, then list various personal "gestures of gratitude" we can make to God.

PRAYER   (6-7 minutes)

Silence   (5 minutes)

It's a good idea to begin the time of silence the same way each week so that group members know what to expect. Ringing a bell or using a similar signal is one way; another way is to read Scripture. This week you might use Psalm 139:23-24 or Psalm 57:7-9 (see Windows, pp. 98-99).

Spoken Prayer   (1-2 minutes)

As usual, close the time of silence with your own prayer or that of someone in your group (ask him or her before your meeting time). A suggested prayer:

> *O God,*
> *rouse us to thanksgiving*
> *because we belong to your family.*
> *Wake the sleeper in us*
> *and kindle such a fire in our hearts*
> *that we shall never be content*
> *with anything short of you.*
> *Relight in us the flame*
> *of a steady life of prayer.*

> *O God,*
> *Keep open our minds, our souls, our hearts.*
> *Amen.*
> —(Adapted from Douglas Steere,
> *Prayer in the Contemporary World*, p. 4)

LOOKING BACK   (15-20 minutes)

During the past week people have been reading and reflecting on chapter 3. They've also begun praying for five minutes each morning and evening, basing their evening prayer on a list of things for which they were thankful during the day. Give them an opportunity now to discuss with others their experiences with these prayers.

Some group members will have done very little and may be feeling somewhat guilty. Others may have faithfully done the exercises and now feel good . . . or pressured . . . or frustrated. Some may not have been able to write prayers of thanks. (Encourage everyone to try again this week.) Accept whatever is said, and encourage where you can.

If necessary, remind the group how important it is that they speak about their experiences so that others can learn from them. If people say nothing for the entire course, they aren't helping others or themselves. It may help to divide into groups of three for a few minutes; one person from each group can report to everyone on what the small group discussed. Or try the "fish bowl": have four to six people form a circle for discussion (the fish bowl). The rest of the class forms a larger circle around the small circle and listens as the small group discusses. One chair in the small group is left empty; if someone from the larger circle wants to speak, he or she sits in the empty chair. When finished speaking, he or she returns to the larger circle.

Keep the discussion moving, though not forced. Focus on gratitude as a means of praying and on what is happening to group members as a result of the exercises they have been doing.

As I mentioned last time, people often like the thanksgiving part. They may even begin to look for things during the day to add to their thanksgiving list at night. This, of course, is the goal: not only to give thanks for five minutes at night but to have a continual attitude of gratitude that takes *nothing* for granted.

I recall one man describing how he had felt separated from people at work because he was a Christian and they were not. After praying "I belong to God" and after making a list of things for which to give thanks, he began to look differently at his coworkers. He realized that these people also belonged to God, and he felt thankful for them too! He felt closer to them and could relate to them better. It's these kinds of comments that can help people in your group gain new insights. I'm always amazed at how many different experiences people have as they become more aware of their lives and of God through prayer. Prayer can become an attitude we have all day long.

LOOKING AHEAD   (5-10 minutes)

Today we take a second look at gratitude. Chapter 3 discussed one aspect of gratitude—it recognizes a gift. But there's more. Gratitude also calls for a response to that gift—an expression of appreciation or a gesture of gratitude. In today's session use enough of chapter 4 to get this idea across; it will lead nicely into the exercise of contemplating the story of the ten lepers.

As time permits, you might ask the group to talk about the difficult time we often have in expressing our thanks for gifts. Gestures of gratitude are not always easy to make. Limit the discussion to make sure you have time for today's rather long In Session exercise.

EXERCISES   (30 minutes)

In Session

This exercise is similar in style to the exercise in chapter 2 that used the story of the prodigal son (see instructions there). Exercises of this kind can be used with many stories in the Bible. They're one more form of "prayer" and meditation on Scripture.

Group members usually find this particular exercise revealing and helpful. Use a bell or music to end each five-minute segment of the exercise.

After allowing fifteen minutes to complete the exercise, go back over it, one part at a time, recording responses on your board or on newsprint. Abbreviate answers as much as possible—people can give a sentence or two of explanation, if necessary.

The answers to "Why didn't you thank Jesus?" may give insight into why we don't give thanks to God. They will not necessarily be bad reasons—good actions and attitudes can also interfere or prevent us from giving thanks. Consider some answers I've heard:

I simply followed the instructions: "Go to the priest," and then, since my home was so close, I went right there. And I celebrated!
I had a family—husband and children—that I hadn't seen for a long time. So I ran home to be with them.
I got busy, but I will go back sometime. (Maybe Jesus won't be there when I get back.)
I was too amazed, overwhelmed. I spent the time telling other people about it.
I went off by myself to think about it.
I wanted to give a gift in kind, but couldn't think of one.
I was angry. "Why hadn't this happened before?" I deserved to be healed.
I was afraid
 — of the power I had experienced.
 — that if I went back I'd have to pay.
 — that he might ask for a commitment. I wasn't ready for any obligations.
I was afraid that it wouldn't last. I felt insecure. Maybe the disease would come back in a day or two.
I was skeptical. "Who knows what really happened? Maybe Jesus had nothing to do with it all. Maybe it was my faith. I don't know."

After you and the group make a list, look back over it and point out that there may be seemingly good reasons for not giving thanks. At any rate, the list is bound to contain reasons—plausible or not—that we use every day. (You may want to read "The Ten Lepers" in *The Way of the Wolf* by Martin Bell. It will help you lead this part of the session.)

Now list responses to the second question: "Why did you return? What was it like?" Again, some responses I've heard:

I was a Samaritan, so I felt I had to thank Jesus.
It heightened my experience of going home to my family and celebrating. I went home more joyful.
I wanted to respond, to make Jesus happy. (Is God happy when we say thanks?)
It was a gift from beyond, but Jesus was nearer so I thanked him.
I had prayed about my disease often and knew the healing came from the One to whom I had prayed. I wanted Jesus to know that I knew.
It made a real personal connection with Jesus. I wanted to be with him even more. I made a commitment to find ways to spend time with him.
I was so amazed, I wanted to share my joy with Jesus.
I was sent back as a representative of the whole group.

After you've compiled a list like this, indicate that there are many reasons for us to give thanks. We receive the gift whether we say thank you or not, but saying thanks enhances our relationship with God.

I hope you have time left to record some of the specific ways we can give thanks (part 3 of the exercise). This can be fun! Here's a list of gestures of gratitude that people in my classes have listed:

Smile
Shout
Tithe
Serve
Laugh
Dance
Play music
Listen
Love
Pray

Walk
Sleep
Take care of self
Touch someone in pain
Do something for someone (even if it's difficult)
Cook, bake
Give Christ credit
Acknowledge Creator
Write thank-you notes
Share thanks with others
Be thankful for others—show them
Enjoy self with a friend
BE
Write a poem to God
Say thanks to God
Spend more time with God
Increase my understanding of God
Study
Get to know Jesus better (like reading the gospels)
Write a letter
Make a phone call
Forgive
Use my talents
Grow
Risk
Meet someone's eyes
Hug
Be happy
Sing
Kneel
Play
Tutor
Visit
Hospitality
Be open and listen to God's Word
Obey
Praise
Share money

Consider taking the list home with you and typing it up for distribution next week. I've found that group members appreciate having the list for their personal reflection. Also, next week you'll be talking about the nature of prayer; the list may be useful in demonstrating how prayer is not only an attitude but also a series of widely divergent acts.

If you run out of time, postpone discussion of part 3 of the In Session exercise until next week's session.

At Home

Read through the instructions, noting that our weekly prayer discipline is taking on slightly more structure and content. I think it's good that people get an idea of what morning and evening prayer—in the Reformed tradition—is like. Actually, it's very similar to such prayers in other traditions, such as Catholic, Anglican, and Lutheran. People may find it a bit stiff at first, but remind them that what we're trying to do is to develop a rather formal discipline of prayer. Later, they'll be able to form their own discipline, perhaps without such a rigid structure.

Especially encourage everyone, then, to faithfully practice the new schedule of morning and evening prayers. Note that participants should continue writing "I am thankful for . . ." as part of their evening prayers. Note, too, that all group members should repeat the contemplation of the story of the ten lepers, again listing personal gestures of gratitude.

PRAYER   *(10 minutes)*

You may want to end the session today with the form of prayer we are asking people to do at home:

Invocation: Leader: *O Lord, open my lips,*
                People: *And my mouth shall proclaim*
                          your praise.

                or, if evening:

                Leader: *O God, come to my assistance,*
                People: *O Lord, make haste to help me.*
Psalm: *Your choice or Psalm 116*
           (see p. 72 of textbook)
Prayer: *Silence for reflection on the psalm.*
           Prayer of thanks.
           Lord's Prayer in unison.

PRAYER AS ATTITUDE: THE GRATEFUL HEART

PURPOSE

Session 5 reviews experiences with the structured prayers suggested as home exercises last week. We may also discuss additional gestures of gratitude and offer reactions to time during the session that we spent in silence.

The rest of the session is aimed at broadening students' concepts of prayer, looking especially at prayer as an attitude of a grateful heart.

PRAYER   (5-7 minutes)

Silence   (5 minutes)

Begin as you have before.

At some point in today's session it might be good to ask the group about their reactions to the opening time of silence. Some people in my group felt they could come late to meetings since, "It doesn't matter anyway; all we're doing is having some silence. We won't miss anything." Others have found silence to be a very relaxing, quieting way to begin, "one of the few times I am silent during the week." Since silence is part of this course, most people feel it's OK. Others, however, might think silence is a waste of time outside of class!

When you solicit reactions to the silence, you might remind the group of its purposes. This silence is a gift of our valuable time to God—not as a means of getting something in return, but as an expression of the total gift of ourselves to God (see Thomas Merton, *Thoughts in Solitude*, p. 103). The silence also helps make us open, vulnerable to God. We are "doing nothing" so God can come to us, can give the Holy Spirit to us. As Henri Nouwen says,

[Silence] is a way of being empty and useless in the presence of God and so of proclaiming our basic belief that all is grace and nothing is simply the result of hard work. . . . In fact, it unmasks the illusion of busyness, usefulness, and indispensability.
—*The Living Reminder*, p. 52

Thus silence can be time to "be still before the Lord and wait patiently for him" (Ps. 37:7). These words are not meant to sound vague and mysterious, but to encourage people to enter silence expectantly, to see it as a meaningful context and condition for prayer.

Practicing the silence in class will show people that they can be silent and that silence has value.

Spoken Prayer   (1-2 minutes)

You know the specific needs of your group by now. A prayer for those needs would certainly be appropriate. Or say the words of the hymn "Take My Life and Let It Be" (see page 82 of the textbook).

LOOKING BACK   (15 minutes)

Ask group members for their reactions to the expanded morning and evening prayers they were asked to do during the week. Did they find the structure helpful or confining? It may be good to remind ourselves that our goal is to build a rather formal discipline of prayer. Before long, people will be putting together their own discipline and may or may not want to use my structure. Note, however, that even the structure I've outlined has a certain amount of built-in flexibility.

Return to last week's topic of specific ways we can express our thanks to God. If you ran out of time last week, take time now to discuss this exercise. If you took the suggestion to type out the list that you and the group made last week, distribute it and read through it together. Maybe group members have some new items to add to the list based on their experiences during the week. Have them save the lists for reference later in the session.

LOOKING AHEAD (10 minutes)

It is prayer as an *attitude* that we will explore this week. Prayer is an act, many acts. But behind it is an attitude. We've been exploring this attitude as we talked about belonging to God and about gratitude as a life response to that belonging. Chapter 5 tries to make us even more conscious of this attitudinal view of prayer, looking especially at the concept of *heart*. In your presentation today, try to broaden our concept of prayer as an attitude of a grateful heart; then, in the exercise, explore what prayer means to us personally.

You could move from the previous discussion of gestures of thanks to prayer as thankfulness by quoting the Heidelberg Catechism, Q&A 116 (see p. 110 of textbook). Bring out that thankfulness is an *attitude* of receptivity. And the place of that receptivity is the heart. (You may want the group to read the first three paragraphs or so of the Reflection for chapter 5.)

I realize that *heart* is a nebulous concept. But it is so important in the Bible and whenever we talk about spirituality in almost any tradition—certainly in the Reformed tradition. So spend some time talking about the heart as you discuss the attitude of prayer. Stress three things: heart is the place where (a) faith begins, (b) God meets us, and (c) we resonate with God. And point out how the attitude of prayer is rooted in a biblical belief in the Triune God. (See chapter 5, Reflection.)

If you wish, ask participants to say all the things that the word *heart* brings to mind, to see how rich the term is, before you give some of the biblical insights. And take time to read at least a couple of biblical passages of your choice (see Windows for a large selection).

EXERCISES (15 minutes)

In Session

1. You can initiate the discussion about prayer by asking people to take a couple of minutes to write down at least three or four words or phrases that come to mind whenever they hear the word *prayer*. Then have each person read his or her list, recording what they say on a blackboard or newsprint to give the group an idea of how broad the concept of *prayer* can be. I know my view of prayer has been expanded by people in my group. Here are some answers I've heard to the question: "What is prayer to me?"

communion
listening
loving
talking to God
openness
satisfaction
answers
caring
communication with God
giving thanks
asking for guidance
acts of kindness
petition
praise
moving from negative to positive attitudes
time out
time out with God
humility
oneness
sharing a burden
quietness
getting in touch with inner self
adjusting my life
reaching out for God's power
self-expression
receiving God's blessing
peace
confession
searching
happy talk
sharing

knowing
being understood
freedom
endurance
trusting
emotions
mental struggling
understanding
repentance
asking
dancing
insight
wisdom
music

You may want to compare the group's list describing prayer to the list of gestures of gratitude (which you distributed earlier in this session). Very likely some items will appear on both lists. If so, that's a good way to show that prayer is both attitude and act (which is the topic for next week's session—see chapter 6). This could even lead to a wider and deeper understanding of what prayer can mean for the way we live.

2. This discussion of "To whom do you pray?" is intended to encourage people to be more intentional in their prayers. Over the years as I've led small groups and retreats, I've found that as we talk about what prayer means to us, *to whom we pray* has also become an important and provocative question. Many people said they pray to "God" in a very general way, and that the name or image of God they use has only a general connection with the specifics of their prayer. In my own unscientific listening to public prayers, I hear "Almighty" and "Father" used most often.

Have group members write down some of their favorite (or most used) names or images of God that they use in prayer. Then share responses and talk about how these names or titles are meaningful to those who use them. I suggest you also talk about how we can expand our images of God. For example, when we feel anxious or sad, calling on God as Comforter or Refuge may be more helpful than addressing God as Creator or Almighty. When we feel weak or helpless, addressing God as

Rock, Strength, or Almighty may encourage us. When we need to talk out a problem, make a decision, or share a joy, speaking to God as Parent or Friend can help us be open and candid. When we are filled with praise for the beauty of nature, addressing God as Creator or Artist may help focus our prayer.

The Bible—especially the book of Psalms—is filled with names and images of God that could help us expand the names and images by which we envision and call on our multifaceted God. You may want to review some of these with your group.

I have often found this entire discussion to be very moving; in fact, it could take up an entire session!

At Home

Read through the new assignment and comment that the commitment is becoming a little more challenging this week: we are asked to expand the structure we've been using to include reading and reflecting on Scripture. We can choose a book that's short enough to read in one week—an epistle of John or Paul; Jude, Esther, Ruth, Jonah, and so on.

Again, remind the group to continue the "I am thankful for . . ." exercise as part of their evening prayers.

PRAYER   *(5-10 minutes)*

You may want to end the session with the form of prayer that people are asked to do at home this week:

> **Invocation:** *(use either morning or evening invocation, as appropriate)*
> **Psalm:** *100 or 116 or a psalm from Windows*
> **N.T. reading:** *Luke 17:11-19 or other passage*
> **Prayer:** *Silence.*
> *Sentence prayers of thanks by group members.*
> *Lord's Prayer in unison.*
> **Hymn:** *"When I Survey the Wondrous Cross" (see p. 84 of textbook)*

SESSION 6

PRAYER AS ACT

PURPOSE

Session 6 first asks us to react to the expanded prayer schedule we've been practicing during the past week. Specific attention is paid to removing barriers to prayer, to improving the prayer discipline.

Looking ahead to prayer as act, we discuss the necessity of a specific time/place for prayer and use of the psalms in prayer. Finally, we each write a personal discipline of prayer, to be practiced at home during the coming week.

PRAYER   *(7-9 minutes)*

Silence   *(5-6 minutes)*

Begin as you have for the past few weeks. Perhaps, now that people are used to the idea, you'll want to add a minute to this time of silence. I usually write (on a board or newsprint) what the schedule for this section is. For example:

7:25   Arrive
7:30   Bell begins silence
7:36   Spoken prayer

Posting a schedule like this avoids having to break the silence with explanations.

Spoken Prayer   *(2-3 minutes)*

Consider asking a group member to lead in prayer. Or sing one of the hymns that mean a lot to the group.

LOOKING BACK   *(10-15 minutes)*

Allow plenty of time for group members to react to the expanded morning and evening prayers they were asked to do during the week. Did they find time for the readings from Psalms and other Scriptures? Were these readings helpful? Talk specifically about

any barriers individuals felt as they attempted to hold to the new prayer discipline. I've found that group members can often help each other overcome difficulties. If nothing else, it's comforting to know that you're not the only one who's struggling! Identifying difficulties (and successes) is doubly important today because group members will soon be asked to write a *realistic* prayer discipline for themselves. Knowing one's strengths and weaknesses is a definite help in writing such a discipline.

You may also want to ask group members if any of them experienced anything during the week that expanded their idea of prayer. Last week, you recall, we discussed how prayer is both an attitude and a variety of acts; perhaps someone can add to the list of what prayer is.

LOOKING AHEAD   *(10-15 minutes)*

Have the group page through chapter 6 and explore with you the act of prayer—the need for a specific time and place for prayer, the various forms of prayer, and the use of psalms in prayer. You might read some sentences from the text and ask for brief reactions as you do so. Examples:

1. "We need to stop often for the act of prayer" (p. 112). Ask for some examples of times when group members pray. Do they find it helpful to set aside a specific time each day (night) for prayer?
2. "Some places more quickly remind us of God or put us in a reverent attitude" (p. 113). What places do group members find especially conducive to prayer?
3. "We need to be silent in order to be attuned to the quiet God" (p. 114). How do they create space for

silence? Is it difficult or easy for them to be silent in God's presence?

4. "I am simply suggesting that we recapture the richness of the psalms in our private and public worship. . . . We find in the psalms a guide for bringing our thoughts to God" (p. 117). Ask the group to discuss their experiences with the psalms. As time permits, ask group members to mention verses from the psalms that have helped them pattern their prayers.

EXERCISES   *(30-35 minutes)*

In Session

Use statement 1 as a quick review of the various forms of prayer that you've practiced so far in this course. The group may be surprised at how many different ways they have been praying. After giving the group opportunity to add other forms of prayer they've been practicing, take some time to discuss which forms seem most helpful to them personally. This will lead into question 2 and the main exercise of this session.

Read the brief explanation of planning a prayer discipline (question 2). Stress that the discipline be one they can follow *realistically* for one week. Point out that establishing a personal prayer discipline is what we have been working toward since session 1. Now each person is asked to make some decisions and commitments about prayer.

Give the group about fifteen minutes to complete the exercise, each person working individually. When finished, break the group into pairs, asking each pair to share their plans for the prayer discipline. In this way, everyone will be accountable to someone for actually doing the discipline at home this week. Next week the pairs will get together and report how things went. It may also be possible for persons to encourage each other during the week.

At Home

The main activity of the week is to put into practice the prayer discipline outlined in today's session (above). People should come ready to discuss and critique what they did, with possible revision of their disciplines in mind.

Besides assigning the usual readings in the chapter, encourage group members to write psalms at home this week.

PRAYER   *(5 minutes)*

If time permits, perhaps group members could write psalms now and use them as the closing prayer (see the form on p. 117 in chapter 6).

Or you could end the session by asking for encouragement from God as the people commit themselves to their personal prayer disciplines.

You could close by having the group sing "My God, Is Any Hour So Sweet" from page 130 in the textbook.

SESSION 7

WRESTLING WITH GOD

PURPOSE

During this session we will discuss and evaluate our personal prayer disciplines. Revisions in our disciplines may be made, as necessary. We will be encouraged to practice our revised disciplines for the next month.

We will then look at prayer as "wrestling with God." After reading examples from Scripture, we will each write our own "psalm of complaint" and discuss how we personally handle feelings of anger and disappointment with God.

PRAYER   *(8-10 minutes)*

Silence   *(7 minutes)*

Note the suggested increase in time. Tell the group about this change before the silence begins so they won't think you've fallen asleep!

Spoken Prayer   *(1-3 minutes)*

Perhaps you could use a psalm as your opening prayer. See chapter 6 for examples, or choose your own.

LOOKING BACK   *(25-30 minutes)*

Today we will be evaluating and revising our prayer disciplines. Since everyone will be encouraged to practice these revised disciplines for the next month or so, today's evaluation and revisions are crucial.

Begin by pairing off the persons who shared their prayer disciplines at the end of last week's session. Ask the pairs to discuss their success in practicing the disciplines they had outlined for themselves; notes from the journals may come in handy for this. The pairs should talk about what changes they would like

to make in their prayer disciplines: more or less time; different place; different forms of prayer; fewer readings; and so on. Allow about ten minutes for discussion.

Then give another five or ten minutes for persons to individually rewrite their prayer disciplines into something they believe they can practice for the next month. The revised disciplines can be written into their journals. Of course, some group members may want to make no changes whatever. But you'll probably find that most people will feel the need to revise, especially since they'll be committing themselves to practicing the discipline for a solid month.

Finally, gather everyone together to share insights that came from the discussion and from the previous week of practicing their disciplines at home. I find it usually helps everyone to hear others comment on their joys and their problems.

LOOKING AHEAD   *(15-20 minutes)*

Today you'll be introducing a topic not always discussed among Christians—wrestling with God. But if we read the Psalms and other Scriptures, we often find the best of God's people struggling with the divine Majesty.

You could begin the presentation by reading some of the Scriptures quoted in chapter 7. How much you read will depend on how much time you have. The idea is to give a biblical background for later discussion. Here is a suggested procedure:

- Start with **Genesis 32:22-32**, the passage about Jacob wrestling with God (from which the title of the chapter comes—see p. 140 of the textbook).

- As the group looks at *At Eternity's Gate* on page 135, ask someone to read **Job 3:11-13, 16** (see p. 141).
- As the group looks at *Woman Weeping* (p. 143) or *Reach* (p. 149), ask someone to read **Jeremiah 20:14-15, 18** ("Cursed be the day . . . spend my days in shame"—see p. 142).
- As the group looks at *Our Lord in the Garden of Olives* (p. 146), ask someone to read **Psalm 22:1-2** ("My God . . . find no rest"—see p. 147) and/or **Mark 15:33-37** (see p. 147).
- Conclude with some appropriate music (perhaps something on Psalm 130—"Out of the Depths") or have a time of silence.

After the readings, briefly present some thoughts from the Reflections of chapter 7. There's no need to discuss any of this now; that will come later in the session.

As you prepare for this presentation, remember that some Christians will object to the whole idea of voicing all our feelings—including anger—to God. Such persons may be reluctant to write a psalm of complaint (see Exercises) and to ever admit to feeling angry or disappointed with God. Something in their theology or personality or training may not allow them to question God, let alone raise a fist to God. Accept that as their spiritual experience. You may invite them to simply listen to the Scriptures, readings, and comments of their classmates. Point out that for some Christians wrestling with God is an authentic act of prayer. Remind those who object that perhaps at some point in the future they too may have feelings of anger, hurt, and disappointment with God. Perhaps even now they may be able to help someone else who is angry or upset with God.

Assure the group that your intent is not to force people to be angry with God when they are not. Rather, the intent is to allow Christians to express feelings that they often suppress. The intent is to help people understand that if our relationship with God is an intimately personal relationship, then there will be struggle as well as joy—just as there is in any personal relationship.

EXERCISES (15-20 minutes)

In Session

1. People have already done this during the "Looking Back" part of this session.
2. If people have been writing psalms of their own at home, the exercise will go easier. In any event, simply ask people to fill in the blank with some questions or complaints to God (see chapter 6 for comments on psalm writing). Then move into a general discussion of the whole experience of "wrestling" with God. See the next question.
3. If group members seem reluctant to describe their experiences of wrestling with God, perhaps you could encourage their participation by giving a personal example of your own. Then spend some time talking about the issue, perhaps along the lines suggested in question 2. Keep in mind the Scriptures read in today's session, Scriptures in which some of God's leading people loudly complain!

   It also helps to expand this discussion beyond anger or confrontation to include decision-making situations that involve confusion or anxiety. In fact, you could even begin the discussion there.

At Home

1. A month may sound like a long time to practice the same prayer discipline. So take a couple of minutes to encourage everyone to give it their best try. Personally, I've found it's not at all helpful to change the prayer discipline every day or two; it takes time (like a month!) to fully appreciate a discipline and to know what its strengths and weaknesses are. Encourage group members to jot their reactions to the discipline in their journals; then, after a month, they can make any changes that seem necessary. In the process some wrestling with God is bound to happen.
2. Because people are practicing a fairly rigorous prayer discipline, they may find themselves hard-pressed for time to read the chapters. Such reading and reflection continues to be an important part of the course, especially for group discussion and personal understanding.

PRAYER

(5-10 minutes)

Read Lamentations 3:21-26, beginning with "All this I take to heart" (see p. 150 of textbook). After a few moments of silent reflection, sing with the class "What a Friend We Have in Jesus" (p. 151).

SESSION 8

PRAYER AND JUSTICE/COMPASSION

PURPOSE

During this session we will express our reactions to chapter 7 and its focus on wrestling with God. We will also discuss our progress with our prayer disciplines.

Looking ahead to chapter 8, we'll hear how prayer and justice/compassion presuppose each other and how the closer we get to God, the closer we come to the suffering people of our world. A time for evening prayers focusing on justice and compassion closes the session.

PRAYER   (10 minutes)

Silence   (8 minutes)

A minute has been added to this week's suggested time for silence. You'll want to inform the class of this change before the silence begins.

Spoken Prayer   (2 minutes)

You may want to read the words of "What A Friend We Have in Jesus" (see p. 151 of the textbook). This was the suggested closing hymn for your last session; using it now will be effective repetition.

LOOKING BACK   (15-20 minutes)

Since we've been reading and reflecting about wrestling with God, it's important to continue this discussion. Perhaps you could read one of the selections from Windows to focus the topic once again. (I use a Scripture passage or something from Nouwen or L'Engle, while people look at *Reach* (p. 149) or other drawings in chapter 7. Then ask group members for reactions. What did they think of the treatment of

↓
pg 147.

wrestling with God in chapter 7? Has anyone any personal experiences of "God-wrestling" to report?

I've found that the older persons in my classes usually understand and appreciate this topic more than younger persons. The older we get, the more experience we have with life's struggles, it seems. Keep in mind the comments of last week regarding persons who do not appreciate the idea of expressing anger and disappointment with God.

After your discussion, take ten minutes to check on progress and problems with the personal prayer disciplines. You can do this as a large group or, if you prefer, discuss in pairs as we did last week. Follow-up is important: some people may be on the verge of quitting their disciplines and may urgently need encouragement; others may be eager to share their successes. Do provide time for this mutual encouragement. Remember that establishing a personal prayer practice is the basic goal of this course.

LOOKING AHEAD   (10-15 minutes)

Remind the group that we are still discussing acts of prayer, this time focusing on prayer as justice and compassion. Introduce the topic by reading aloud the story of Agathon and the three paragraphs that follow it (pages 158-159 of the textbook). Note especially the lines that express the theme of chapter 8: "Prayer presupposes justice and compassion. But justice and compassion also presuppose prayer." If you wish, read a Scripture passage or two to further establish the theme (see Matt. 5:23-24, for example).

Then spend some time making some observations about our topic—prayer and justice/compassion. I usually point out that now we are contemplating our neighbors—those close to us and those more distant brothers and sisters whom we label "the poor, the oppressed, the suffering, the hungry." When we pray for such people, we reach out to those whom we may not be able to name but whom our faith tells us are loved by God. Such persons elicit the compassion of Christ. And if our prayer is sound, it must empower and nurture such love and compassion in our hearts.

I believe that today's topic is crucial, though it is often left out of discussions about spirituality and prayer. Social activists sometimes think people concerned about prayer and the inner life tend to avoid the tough questions of life in a sinful world. A concern for spirituality can lead to spiritual selfishness and narcissism. On the other hand, contemplative people have accused activists of superficiality and shallow spiritual commitment. This chapter is an attempt to bring these two necessary aspects of the Christian life together so that we will build prayer habits that sustain our societal love and commitment; our societal commitment will be a kind of contemplation of God's love for all people in need. Please make sure today that group members realize prayer loses much of its dynamic if this concern for justice and compassion is missing. (For a more complete discussion of "Contemplating People and Society," see *Noisy Contemplation* by William R. Callahan, S.J., pp. 8, 14- 16, 18-20.)

EXERCISES AND PRAYER
(25-30 minutes)

In Session

The exercise today takes us through "evening prayers" designed to expand concepts of contempla-

tion. So far we've been contemplating Scripture, God, things to be thankful for, our feelings, and so on. This exercise invites us to include family, neighbors, and the world in our contemplation. This is not to say, of course, that so far all our contemplation has been centered on self. But now we turn deliberately toward others and consciously expand our prayer and contemplation.

The format of the exercise is clear enough. Our prayers for others constitute the heart of the exercise: Ask the group to sit in silence with an attitude of prayer as you quietly announce the various categories of people (family, friends, enemies, poor, oppressed, etc.) for whom they can silently pray.

Please note that this prayer and the hymn that follow constitute the "closing prayer" for today's session.

At Home

Support people in practicing their prayer disciplines at home. Ask them to include prayers of compassion and justice this week, as suggested in the exercise. Remind them to continue finding time during the day for reading and reflecting on the materials in chapter 8.

Finally, encourage people to contemplate the news.

SESSION 9

THE GOAL IS GLORY

PURPOSE

The session begins by reviewing our experiences of praying for those in need of justice and compassion. The importance and benefits of such prayers are reiterated.

The final chapter of the course, "The Goal Is Glory," is introduced along with its theme—that it's our joy and lifelong goal to bring glory to our God. We then contemplate the transfiguration and write a prayer of praise based on that contemplation.

PRAYER   (11-14 minutes)

Silence   (9 minutes)

You might add an additional minute of silence today so that by the end of the course (next week) group members will be spending ten minutes in silence.

Spoken Prayer   (2-5 minutes)

Perhaps you could again ask for spoken prayers from group members for those in special need of justice and compassion (see last week's In Session exercise for examples).

LOOKING BACK   (10-15 minutes)

To help people recall their experiences with intercessory prayer, read the entry for Monday from Henri Nouwen's *The Genessee Diary* (see p. 164 of textbook). Nouwen notes that "in praying for others, I lose myself and become the other." Ask if group members experienced this as they offered intercessory prayers for others during the past week.

Take time to explore other reactions with the group. For example, did people feel drawn closer to God as they prayed for others? Did they feel impelled toward some kind of direct action or service as a result of praying earnestly for the poor, the hungry, the lonely? Did their prayers help them hear the cries of the needy more distinctly?

Perhaps you can share this paragraph from Hughes Oliphant Old's book *Praying with the Bible*. It offers some helpful suggestions about what should be included in our prayers of intercession:

> There are certain things that should always be included in our prayers of intercession. We should always pray first for the church, for our own local church, as well as for churches throughout the world. We should pray for the peace, unity, and purity of the church. (See John, ch. 17.) Second, we should pray for the ministry of the gospel; for pastors, teachers, elders, and deacons; for evangelists, missionaries, church administrators, and especially for our own pastor. (Eph. 6:19; Col. 4:2.) Third, we should pray for all people, particularly those who have not received the gospel. (1 Tim. 2:1-8.) Fourth, we should pray for our President and all those in authority in our nation, as well as for those world leaders who are responsible for maintaining peace and justice (vs. 2-4). Fifth, we should pray for all those who suffer or are in special need, particularly those of our friends and neighbors whose specific needs are known to us (James 5:13-16).
>
> —Hughes Oliphant Olds,
> *Praying with the Bible*, p. 88

Finally, speak some words of encouragement to any who may be struggling with their weekly prayer disciplines. Group members have completed—if on schedule—three weeks of their personal disciplines. Next week, as they begin their second month of practicing prayer at home, they may want to make some adjustment in their disciplines.

LOOKING AHEAD   (10 minutes)

To introduce the final chapter of *Space for God,* you might start by reading John 17:4-6, 8-10 (see p. 185); then talk about how the glory of Christ can shine through us and how God's glory is the goal of the spiritual life. The central question of life, for the Calvinist, is simply this: "How shall God be glorified?"

The selection by Smedes (see p. 193) may also be helpful in capturing what it means to be a God-glorifier. Perhaps the people in your group share Smedes's feeling that it takes a long time to like the notion of being a God-glorifier. Solicit their reactions to the idea of living with the single purpose of bringing glory to God.

EXERCISES   (30 minutes)

In Session

For the third (and final!) time during this course, I suggest you use the contemplation approach to Scripsure, this time focusing on transfiguration of Christ (Luke 9:29-36—see p. 183). The object of the contemplation is to help us sense Jesus' great transforming glory, to see again the glory of God in a person, a human being. Seeing Jesus, the Light of the World, in this way reminds us of how his glory can shine through us and glorify God.

If the group has forgotten some of the details of "contemplating" a Bible story, a few reminders are in order. Check sessions 2 or 4 for instructions for using this method.

After the group has finished this meditation, take time to discuss some of their reactions. Following are a few of the things people in my groups have said about this experience:

I hardly dared imagine being there.
My faith was deepened by being reminded of Jesus' divinity.
It was too wonderful. I didn't feel like I belonged there. Why would I be chosen to experience all that?
It reminded me of a time I felt very close to God.
I can understand why the disciples were silent, or why Peter said dumb things—I didn't know what to say.
I can't see why the disciples didn't tell anyone. I wanted to tell everyone I saw!
People would think I was crazy if I told them what happened. They wouldn't believe it. How did I know that it was Moses and Elijah?
I imagine that it was an experience something like at Easter.

You may want to save the prayers of praise for your closing prayer.

At Home

Remind the group to think about any revisions they might want to make in their personal prayer disciplines. Encourage them to come next time with specific ideas for change, if necessary. After next time, they'll be on their own with their revised disciplines.

PRAYER   (5-10 minutes)

Ask for volunteers to share the prayers they wrote as part of the contemplation exercise. Or, if you prefer, sing a hymn that has become a favorite of the group.

SESSION 10

A LOOK BACK, A LOOK AHEAD (CONCLUSION)

PURPOSE

This final session offers us a chance to look back at chapter 9 and its theme of glorifying God, at what we've learned from this course, and at our prayer disciplines.

We then look ahead toward continuing our (revised) prayer disciplines for at least another month. A psalm of praise from each of us concludes the course.

PRAYER   *(12-15 minutes)*

Silence   *(10 minutes)*

Ten weeks ago you began by observing one minute of silence—and perhaps that seemed long to some group members. Today you and your group can savor ten minutes of quiet meditation. Since this is likely the last regular meeting, prayer today can be especially precious and meaningful.

Spoken Prayer   *(2-5 minutes)*

Give thanks for each member of your group by name. Or read a psalm of praise to God, perhaps from chapter 9.

LOOKING BACK   *(30-40 minutes)*

To reestablish the theme of chapter 9, try reading one or more psalms of praise. (The chapter offers selections from Psalm 96, 98, 148, and 150.) Group members might take turns reading verses from these—or other—psalms. Follow the readings with some discussion of reactions to chapter 9.

As part of their "look back," group members ought to evaluate their personal prayer disciplines, especially since they've now practiced—or attempted to

practice—their disciplines for one full month and are about to embark on a second month. You could ask group members to pair off, perhaps with the same person with whom they shared their progress earlier in the course. Give the pairs about ten minutes to talk about what changes, if any, they would like to make in their prayer disciplines: more or less time, different place, different forms of prayer, fewer readings, and so forth. Then allow another five or ten minutes for persons to individually rewrite their prayer disciplines into something they believe they can practice for the next month. The revised disciplines can be written into the journals. Of course, some group members may want to make no changes whatsoever, but others will want to revise, especially since they'll be committing themselves to practice the discipline for another month.

You may also want the group to "look back" on what they learned from the course. Discuss what was most helpful or meaningful and what could be changed and improved. I would be grateful if you'd pass your comments along to CRC Publications, 2850 Kalamazoo Ave., Grand Rapids, Michigan 49560.

LOOKING AHEAD   *(10 minutes)*

The main thing to accomplish during this time is to encourage group members to faithfully follow their prayer disciplines for another month. Perhaps you can share some encouraging Scriptures with the class. Or group members may be helped by talking about their personal prayer disciplines: what do they intend to do, when, where, and so forth? Encourage people to develop a realistic plan and then stick to it.

It may help the group considerably if they know you're planning another group meeting at some point in the future. (I try to meet again in a month.) At that follow-up session, we can talk about our progress and can encourage each other. If such a get-together is impractical, maybe participants could meet informally with a friend from the group as a means of helping each other grow spiritually and stick to the prayer disciplines.

EXERCISES

No exercises are listed for this session, either here or in the textbook. The only At Home exercise for group members is continued practice of our individual prayer disciplines.

PRAYER   *(10-15 minutes)*

Give each group member about five minutes to write a psalm of praise ("I praise you, God, for . . ."). Conclude the course by asking each person to read his or her psalm of praise.

A personal note from the author:

We have completed our short journey together. I hope your life has been broadened and deepened a little as you led this course. I hope that your time together as a group has taken some of the terror out of prayer, and either introduced people to the joy of prayer or enhanced the prayer life that some of them already had. May you live your life constantly aware and surprised by the gracious, glorious, invigorating presence of our Triune God—to whom be glory forever and ever. Amen!